A LOOK, SEE AND TOUCH BOOK

Dorothy Edwards

Illustrated by

Peter Edwards

First published in Great Britain 1976
by Methuen Children's Books Ltd
11 New Fetter Lane, London EC4P 4EE
Text copyright © 1976 by Dorothy Edwards
Illustrations copyright © 1976 by Peter Edwards
Printed in Great Britain by
William Clowes & Sons Ltd, Beccles, Suffolk

ISBN 0 416 79250 2

Look, look, this is O. O is round.

this
is
my

this
is
your

We put our fingers on the O, round and round

RIGHT HAND

Round and round...

and round we go.

← LEFT HAND

Round and round.

A plate is round.

An orange is round.

An apple is round.

Let's go round the plate and the orange and the apple.

Here is a round orange
in a round dish.

Here is a round pond
with a round fish.

Touch the fish.

Look, look, here is a cat.

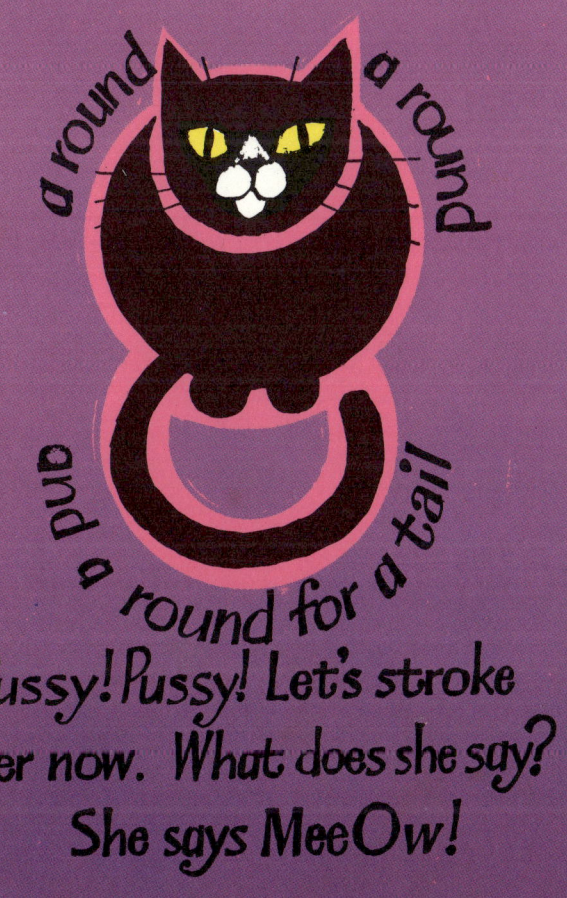

a round a round
a nd a round for a tail

Pussy! Pussy! Let's stroke her now. What does she say? She says MeeOw!

And the fat round puppy dog says BOw-wOw!

Pat him gently.

This round sheep says baa-baa-baa, her round baby lamb says maa-maa-maa.

We go round the

big pig.

Round the small mouse.

This is a round

tree.

A round lady, a round man.

A round boy and girl.

Now: here is a house.
Touch: a window, a window,
a window, a window,
and a door!
Tap, tap, tap on the door.
Tap! Tap! Is anyone at home?
No!
So we will follow
the path,

and go for a finger walk up

Can you find
the round pigs
the sheep and the lambs
and the lady
by her house?
If you look very hard
you will find
the round

mouse.

and round the path.

Over we go...

...to the park.
Can you see
the boy and girl?
Walk to them.

Now let's walk on.
The path leads
back to
the house.

The gate is open.
The door is open.
Come in, come in,
dinner's ready.

This is your round dinner on a round plate.

Round potatoes, round peas and a round fish cake, with a round mug of milk to drink.

A round pudding in a round bowl and a round apple too!

All gone.

No more.